~ 1 ~

GOD MADE MALE & FEMALE

IN HIS IMAGE AND LIKENESS HE CREATED THEM

AUTHOR: DEBORAH LEE SR.

Dedication

I like to dedicate this book to my Lord and Savior Jesus Christ who is the God of my life. He inspired me to write this book so those that are living wrong would live according to His will which is Righteousness. God is always the author to every book I intend to write.

To my parents John and Lillian Lee who raised me to live the life I live now. Mom now deceased told me before she died was to move forward and that she loves me in this I will keep moving on in her memory.

To my wonderful, fascinating; and successful children Regina, Tamika, April, Cj. And Matthew I love you very much and y'all being a part of my life story have made me a strong black woman and I pray that y'all learn from my testimony that God can take a mess and turn it into a blessing.

To my grandchildren Say, Destiny, Samara, Savay, Jamari, BranDon and Sage and to those in the future know that God never fails and He can do anything if you believe. Always look the Him the Author and Finisher of your faith.

To all the Bishops, Pastors and those who I ministered in dance with to those who inspired me keep trusting God and He will surely bring things in your life to past. Thank you for making me the successful woman that I am today and always will be even after this life. I thank God for y'all for being part of my journey in life. Love you.

INTRODUCTION

In the beginning God created the heavens and the earth. When we read the book of Genesis chapter 1& 2 in the KJV we will find the whole story of how the world began. What stuck out to me is when God made man in His image and likeness Chapter 2:7 And the LORD God formed man out of the dust of the ground, and breathed into his nostrils the breath of life; and man became a living soul. This was the first creation of a human being (Man). As we read further in this chapter to vs 18 And He (God) said, it is not good that man should be alone; I will make him an help meet for him. Vs 21 And the LORD God caused a deep sleep to fall upon Adam, and he slept: and He (God) took one of his (Adam) ribs, and closed up the flesh instead thereof; vs22 And the rib, which the LORD God had taken from man, made he a woman, (God's second creation a woman) and brought her unto man. Vs 23 And Adam said, This is now bone of my bones, and flesh o my flesh: she shall be called Woman, because she was taken out of Man. Vs 24 Therefore shall a man leave his father and his mother, and shall cleave unto his wife; and they shall be one flesh. This is the sanctity (a state or quality of being holy, sacred, or saintly, godliness) of what God intended for a man and a woman.

And this is what I will be introducing throughout this book the way God intended for not only the way the world suppose to be like but the intent of a male and Female as God guides me.

I believe that everything God created was and still is good. He made everything after its own kind and blew a kiss upon it. One thing for sure and we can count on is this God never make mistakes for He is to wise and He put everything in its place.

He made man for female and they were made to be fruitful and multiply and on this part is mentioning on procreation; Merriam-Webster Dictionary defines it as to beget or bring forth (offspring) procreate-reproduction and they were to till the land together.

By all means it is not to judge the homosexual, lesbian, and gay; transvestite but to teach the truth on what God words say about it. It is to reveal how the devil has turned what God did for good and he (the devil) turned it around for evil and deceiving many into thinking this is the way God intended the world to be when the word say in (Genesis 50:20 the Amplified Bible) As for you, you thought evil against me, but God meant if for good, to bring about that many people should be kept alive, as they are this day. I gonna say this although Satan turned everything God did to evil God is turning everything back around at its' original state to save this generation that was cursed. Jesus is the answer to all of our sinful state.

The Bible is also to remind us of the responsibility of a male and female role as we're living together under God's ordinance.

The Lord does not delay [as though He were unable to act] and is not slow about His promise, as some count slowness, but is [extraordinarily] patient toward you, not wishing for any to perish but for all to come to repentance 2 Peter 3:9 (the Amplified Version Bibleway.com) not what the enemy is telling or showing how it should be God is saying He don't want you stuck in your mess. I am patiently waiting for you to turn from your wicked way because I don't want you to perish.

The Discussion

When I first was inspired to write this book God and I had a discussion of what to put in it so that it won't offend but deliver. First the people must understand is that this book is not offensive but preventive from sin. It is to show you what hurts God and yes He has feeling and it saddens Him that He see how the world turned out again. The book of Noah, the days of Lot while living in Sodom and Gomorrah is a good read. We see what God is capable of allowing things to happen when we refuse to obey His laws, commands and precepts. God picked out these scripture for you to learn from them as well as get delivered from sin. He speaks to me every time I open my laptop to type what He is saying next. I when God has a message to turn us to Him through His messengers they want to kill us but really don't want to face the truth of God's Word.

This is the kind of relationship God wants with each and every one of us. He has a plan for us here on earth as well have heaven but we can't expect to be with God if we continue in sin. For I know the thoughts that I think towards you, say the LORD, thoughts of peace, and not evil, to give you an expected end. Jer 29:11 (KJV). God wants every man to live in peace away from sin. You see when we do what we think if right we allow all kinds of confusion going on in our lives but when we decide to turn our lives over to God peace come with dwelling in His presence. The peace that surpasses all understanding that guards our hearts and mind. Peace that the world could never give us.

My prayer is that y'all read with the understanding the God loves you and He does not want you to wallow in the state that you're in. He delight is that you be saved and return back home to Him.

GOD MADE MAN IN HIS IMAGE AND LIKENESS

So God created mankind in his own image, in the image of God he created them; male and female Gen 1:27 New International Version NIV)

In the beginning we see that God created everything from the light to creatures the most magnificent thing God created was man (the head). He miraculously made him out of the dust and blew the breath of life into his body and man became a living soul but before this entire world came into existence God, Jesus and the Holy Spirit were having a conversation about us.

(Paraphrasing) He guys look here now y'all saw what I created so how about us creating man in our image and likeness. Jesus and the Holy Spirit that sounds cool. Adam was God first creation that God blew His breath of life into his body and he became a living soul.

The amazing part of this story is God took dust, made it into a man and blew the breath of life in his body; now imagine that man from the dust begin to move. It reminds me of the Sandman in the Spiderman movie when the sand was coming together.

After God did which was good gave Adam specific instructions to name all the animals in the Garden and whatever he named them that was their name (Gen 2:19-20). Then He (God) Adam Authority over the earth in other words he had dominion if you will (Gen 1: 26b).

Adam obeyed God and name each and every one of the animals, took care of the fields but something was missing so God said it is not good for man to be alone (Gen 2:18). God caused a deep sleep to fall upon Adam (Gen 2:21) He (God) took one rib from Adam (right) side (representing God's righteousness and the perfect woman for Adam).

God strategically shaped this woman with everything a one man would desire to have. Closed Adam right side up with flesh, woke Adam up; and was present to him a woman (Gen 2:22a).

I could imagine Adam waking up and seeing this beautiful, shapely creature standing in from of him. His eyes filled with excitement adoring at her.

Someone who fearfully and wonderfully made came from his side. A woman he didn't even know that existed inside his own body. Adam saying (paraphrasing) Wow God "This is bone of my bones and flesh of my flesh; she shall be called Woman because she was taken out of Man.

My study bible from the NKJV say in verse 22 The verb for made mean to build"; The expansion of one's small part into a complete body makes sense in today's understanding of molecular structure and DNA verse 23 **this is now** mean "At Last" bone of my bones. Adam wording is poetic and exalted—seeing Eve was a shocking and exhilarating experience because the match was perfect. Here was a mirror of himself, someone just like him and yet different!

She shall be called Woman: (capital letter representing respect of who Eve was to Adam). In giving the woman her name Adam was functioning as he had in naming the animals (v19). Yet the name he gave her matched his own. She was woman and he was man perfectly suited for each other.

God told Adam whatever you named them that it was so established in heaven so we became Woman as Adam has said because we are a perfect match to a man as you can say the man in the mirror but made different for his use. The one they (God and Adam) have chosen us to be and we are as God attended in (Gen 2:24a) to be Adam's wife.

Male and female was to dwell together has Husband and Wife. It is in the beginning so shall it be in the end. God never and I mean never said anything about a man marrying the same sex or vise versa concerning a woman. This kind of movement it goes against God purpose for male and female. We have stepped over the boundaries of God will for humanity.

You shall not lie with a male as with a woman it is an abomination (Lev 18:22 NKJV study bible)

God word is not condemning you He (God) is simply saying that it is against nature to sleep with the same sex. God doesn't want us indulging in such behavior like I stated earlier this is not the will or plan of God for our lives.

When Adam disobeyed God the whole world fell into utter darkness and everything seem to be right in our eyes never seeing that we were sinning against God. It simply means scales were put over our eyes so we could not see where we were heading. The enemy knows more about us then you think. He deceived Eve to get to the man because God had given Adam authority and Lucifer before he fell was very jealous of God creation so he sent a serpent to beguile Eve to get to Adam. Tore us from God presence and now we have a nation full of sin.

<u>God's Designed</u>

God designed a males body parts to fit the females body parts; let me be transparent here. God gave a man a penis to enter a woman's vagina to reproduce from man seed to woman egg thus producing a baby. It is God's will and way of life nothing is gonna change from this truth.

Although this scripture speaks about adultery let us focus on the man and how he should be satisfied with the wife of his youth-enjoy her for God has equip her with everything a man can desire and guess what it all in one woman so there is no excuse for you (men) to step out on your wives looking for any spoil.

Her breast should always satisfy you whether they're small, medium or large. God made them in different sizes along with the rest of her body in which should captive you and no other woman should be able to turn you on like the beautiful graceful foe that she is.

When she comes in the room your heart should still skip a beat from the first time you meet her until now. It (your heart) should always say My God I thank you for this wonderful woman you have given me that after all these years she still turns me on.

The words said rejoice with the wife of your youth comprise a common and an encouragement to find pleasure in the mutual joy of married love.

Be happy with her. Leap for joy for her. Grow older together and find pleasure in her presence.

Pleasure in the marriage bed is blessed by God. The marriage bed that God is referring to is between a man and a woman. They ought to take pleasure in each other as God intended it to be.

The book of Hebrews chapter 13:4 speaks about the marriage is honorable among all, and the bed undefiled; but fornicators and adulterers God will judge. The bed once again is between a man and a woman making love or getting intimate with each other never allowing anything come between what God has joined. The marriage bed was never made for the same sex that is defile in every form. God calls it an abomination (hatred) at every level.

The bible and Merriam-Webster dictionary has the same meaning of what undefiled means-undefiled not corrupt impure, or unclean, not defiled but the fornicators and adulters God will judge.

Prvb's 5: 18-19 (NKJV) Study Bible

Let the fountains be blessed and rejoice with the wife of your youth v 19 as a loving deer and a graceful foe; let her breast satisfy you at all times

Let's look at the word Fountain

1. An ornamental structure in a pool or lake from which one or more jets of water are pumped into the air. Let's use this in a woman form- an ornamental structure of her body, a pool or lake of shapely curves, breast etc. filled with the goodness for a man; jets of happiness to make a man heart glad as she pumps her love toward him.   That is a blessing when a man find a woman like that and he will forever rejoice in his God

2. Fountain is the symbol of joy and peace. Water is anyway a sign of calmness, and symbolizes relief of situations in life.

3. This is what a woman should bring to a man home when he has had a rough day at work and the man should rejoice in the wife of his youth and be satisfied with her breast only at all times. You cannot get this from the same sex because it is out of God's will.

Men should see the beauty of a woman and why God created her in the first place. The woman is to fulfill the desire of her husband and vice versa. Paul puts it this way But a married man has to think about his earthly responsibilities and how to please his wife (female) 1 Cor 7:33 New Living Translation (NTL). The married woman has to think about her earthy responsibilities and how to please her husband.

Fruitful and Multiply

God speaks on being fruitful and multiply. It is meant for a male and female to come together to procreate the earth anything else is a sin before God eyes. As stated earlier God doesn't condemn He corrects what is wrong. He (God) points out what we need to do in order for us to change our behavior according to His word. If He doesn't show us our sin through His word we will continue to be in utter darkness when He said let there be light Jesus is the light of the world and now that the word has come we can see where we are heading. No man can find his way in utter darkness he will be using his hands to guide him through life but when the light is turned on which is the word it unveils the truth and that truth leads to eternal life. It brings us back to the Father of Lights.

The Flesh Will Fail Us

The Book of Roman Chapter 8 speaks about the flesh and how we are not condemned because of Christ Jesus and we don't follow after the flesh but after the Spirit which is of God. The flesh failed but through Jesus we were made free to live a life sinless for what the law couldn't do God sent His only begotten Son in the likeness of sinful flesh to take the sins of the world upon Him and abolished sin through His blood.

The flesh itself does not mind the thing of God but it want to be satisfied with flesh but those who walk after the Spirit mind the kinds of the Spirit.

Simply put those who live after the flesh love what the flesh has to offer but those who live by the Spirit love the things of the Spirit has to offer which is eternal life as for the flesh which is carnal mind the things of death.

This brings much confusion, sadness, and no peace especially with God. I will not allow anything to separate me from God presence or love for me. We have been made more than conquers to overcome this sinful flesh. No matter what obstacles come my way I will not allow it to come between my God and me.

If we continue to live in the flesh we will reap corruption. Flesh could never glory in God's sight but righteousness will always prevail. This is why the bible says in Gal 6:7 (KJV) be not deceived: God is not mocked: for whatsoever a man soweth, that shall he reap v8 For the that soweth to his flesh shall of the flesh reap corruption; but he that soweth to the Spirit shall of the Spirit reap life everlasting.

If we are living according to what our flesh want and strive on that it bring forth death; a separation from God and His wrath abides with us. But there is hope God wishes for no man to perish. The Lord isn't really being slow about his promise, (Jesus is coming back) as some people think. No, he is being patient for your sake (God is waiting for you to denounce sin) He does not anyone to be destroyed but wants everyone to repent 2 Peter 3: 9 New Living Translation (NTL).

If we decide to trust God and accept Jesus Christ as our Lord and Savior we will live eternally with the Father. Believe God is not mocked whatever He says He means. If we chose Him we chose life if not we chose death away from God for all eternity.

<u>The Wife</u>

I believe God addresses the wife second is because Adam was the head just like He did in the beginning after the fall. He specifically gave Eve her responsibility as Adam's wife. To the woman He said, "I will make your pains in childbearing very severe; with painful labor you will give birth to children. Your desire will be for your husband, and he will rule over you." Gen 3: 16 New International Reader's Version. (NIRV) Ladies the men will rule over us God said it and it is good. Then God addresses the man v17 To Adam He said, "Because you listen to your wife and ate fruit from the tree about which I commanded you 'You must not eat from it,' "Cursed is the ground because of you; through painful toil you will eat food from it all the days of your life v18 it will produce thorns and thistles for you, and you will eat the plants of the field v19 By the sweat of your brow you will eat your food until you return to the ground, since from it you were taken; for dust you will return.

Men your purpose is to go outside of the home and make living to support your wives. You were supply the finances so the wife can supply what the home needed. So if you are going through all kind of issues on the job it was prophesied that you will be aggravated, frustrated and disappointed on a promotion or a raise because you didn't stand in your rightful authority that God placed in Adams' hand.   This is all a man and a woman is to be expected to go through together.

Submission

Instructions for Christian Households

Submit to one another out of reverence for Christ. Vs 23 Wives, submit yourselves to your own husbands as you do to the Lord. V23 For the husband is the head of the wife as Christ is the head of the church, his body, of which he is the Savior vs 24 Now as the church submits to Christ also wives should submit to their husbands in everything. Eph 5:21-24 (New International Version) NIV

To understand what Jesus is meant by wives submitting to their own husband let's find out what submit means so that the wives won't have a problem with this word.

Submit-verb-

1. Accept or yield to a superior force or to the authority or will of another person
2. Similar: give in, yield, and give away

God placed man as the head of us. He was to rule over us not have superior force but with love that would cause us to submit to his authority.

I had a real misunderstanding when my brother and I got in to a quarrel about this man saying on YouTube that we're their property and that they own us. I immediately said nobody owns me but God which is true in 1Cor 6:19.

I had to do my research on what he was talking about and in my research I discovered that in Jewish culture when a man wanted to marry their daughter they had to present something to their girls fathers in order for them to marry them and they became their property. They own them.

In marriage the husband has legal rights over us they do own us. But not in a bad way but as our protectors, provider and security as God intended them to be for us.

The research I've done says "The reason why women have to problem with submitting is because they fear the abuse of such power and with good reason many men have abused this power God had given them over their wives." Leaving them (the wives) disrespecting the good men.

God teaches that when a woman and children willingly submit to the authority of the husband and father in the home-he blesses them and it's a testimony to the world of God's power. This is true when a man is in the right position God places him in the blessing of the Lord falls all around the family as long as he don't relinquish his authority to another like Adam did.

The Husband

"When a husband uses the power God has given him, not for his own sinful and selfish desires but for the glory of God he blesses his entire family through his leadership, provision, and protection." (1 Peter 3: 1-6)

Husbands you ought to love your wives as Christ commanded you too as you love the church and give your life for her to make her holy, cleansing (a) by the washing with water through the word, v 27 and to present her to himself and a radian church, without stain or wrinkle or any other blemish, but holy and blameless v28 In this way, husband ought to love their wives as their own bodies. He who loves his wife loves himself. V29 After all, no one ever hates his own body. V33. However, each one of you must love his wife and he loves himself, and the wife must respect her husband.

Dwelling together in love and respect for one another as Christ has commanded will either bring blessing into the home or curses. Husbands are to make sure they take care of the wives as their own bodies. Keep it clean, teaching the word of God and present her holy before the Lord even in intimacy. That mean respecting her as the woman of God you know she is. You are our protector, security, and providers and a woman need to know that you will always be there for her. Not misusing the authority God has given you.

Jesus is not inferior to the father, but is the second person in the trinity, so wives are equal to their own husbands yet in marriage a husband and wife has different roles to the **Lord**; a wife voluntary submission arises out of her own submission to Christ.

Wives if we submit to Christ and follow Him in everything it would come easy for us to submit to our own husbands (stipulation) as long as they are following Christ and if they lead us down the wrong path they would have to answer to Jesus.

Furthermore, Paul puts it this way as I continue to read my (NKJV) Study bible He doesn't emphasis the husband authority: instead he call on the husband to love self sacrificially. Husbands are to emulate Christ love, the kind of love that is willing to lay down one's life for another person and serve that person even if it means suffering. How many husbands are willing to do that for their wives?

This paragraph is written is referring to husbands and wives for the benefit of clarify what God intention for a male and female to dwell together under His ordinance. How they should be respectful towards one another, equal-walking together as one flesh in love.

Emphasis Husband (male) Wife (female) in a marriage ordained by God suffering and giving for the other person.

If a man lies (sleep, get intimate) with a male as he lies with a woman, both of them have committed an abomination Lev 20:13 (Nelson NKJV Study Bible)

Abomination means-anything that causes disgust or hatred.

Difference between abomination and sin-abomination on the other hands is something that causes anyone disgust or hatred. Sin can be an abomination because sin causes God to be disgusted with our association with evil thoughts. In other words what is not of God does not come from God it comes from the world and its lustful desires, words and deeds.

Abomination as a word sounds like someone has acne some evil that sin (June 13, 2016 http://www.quora.com>what-is-the. What is the difference between Sins and Abomination?-Quora.

Reprobate Scripture—Reprobation in Christian Theology is a doctrine of the bible found in many passages of Scripture such as Rom 1:20-28, Proverbs 1:23, John 12:37-41, and Heb 6:4-8 etc. You can read those scriptures at your leisurely time. Which teaches that a person can reject the gospel to a point where God in turn rejects them and curse the conscience to do unnatural and aboming things?

The English word reprobate is from Latin root probate (English prove, test) and thus derived from the Latin, reprobatus (reprove, condemned), the opposite of approbatus (commended, approved)

When a sinner is so hardened as to feel no remorse or misgiving of conscience it is considered a sign of reprobation. This isn't teaching that because of their wicked actions that God will not save them, but its teaching that God has withdrawn His offer of salvation and He gives them over to a seared conscience and now they can do vile actions.

The vile actions and the many different things are evidence of a reprobate mind.

Disobeying God wanting to continue in sin He will utterly leave us to our destruction. God cannot and will not dwell in sin for He is Holy 1 Peter because it is written "You shall be Holy for I am Holy. Everything God created is Holy even after Adam disobeyed God.

The LORD God does not see a fallen world He sees it as it was from the Beginning at it was good.

When I think back on the days of Lot and Noah how God sent destruction by fire and water He utterly destroyed mankind. It behooved that God made man in His image and likeness just to see them turn around and do the same thing He just destroyed in that time.

I take a step back and see what this world have become and what the legal system have passed a law allowing men to marry the same sex and vise versa. Where is the word of God and Where does it stand in the lives of our jurisdictional system?

The jurisdictional system has fallen from grace and has thrown out In God We Trust out of the court houses. Trying to abolish the name of our God little do they know God is not gonna be silent He will avenge the sinners if that's the way they want to live. The wrath of God is upon the house of the sinners and it will not be removed until they rectify themselves back to God in which He gave His son Jesus as a Proprietor for us. In actuality God does own us and we are His property.

The Head (Males Only)

Adam

1. Made in the image and likeness of God- Gen 1:27

2. Made out from the dust- Gen 2:7

3. God blew the breathe of life in man and became a living soul- Gen 2:7

4. God commanded Adam not to eat from the tree of knowledge of good and evil- Gen 2:17

5. Adam was given dominion over the earth. He named every animal- Gen 1:26, 28

6. God said it's not good for man to be alone- Gen 2:18

7. Adam disobeyed God by eating from the tree of the knowledge of good and evil- Gen 3:6

8. Adam hid from God-Gen 3:8 (although it says they God called out to Adam)

9. Adam the man was punished by God and because of that Adam had to till the land by the sweat of his brow-Gen 3:17-19

Although Adam failed as being the head in t\he kingdom of God by disobeying God by eating from the tree of knowledge of good and evil God still made him the head of his household. He had to work for a living in order to feed his wife Eve. (Gen 3:17-19).

<u>Submissive (Females Only)</u>

The Woman

1. God said let us make mankind in our image in our likeness- Gen 1:26
2. God created them female (not leaving out the male)
3. It's not good for man to be alone. God created a helper suitable for Adam- Gen 2:18 (Woman)
4. God caused a deep sleep to take one rib from Adam's side and made a woman (female) to the man-Gen2:21-22
5. Adam name here woman because she was taken from his body- Gen 2:23
6. The woman was deceived –Gen 3:1-6
7. The woman had to bare children in hard labor and she was to fulfill the desire of her husband (submit) He has rule over her-Gen 3:16

After the fall of man Adam and Eve were cast out of the Garden of Eden to begin a new life together. They became parents of two sons Cain and Able this was the first family between a man and a woman. I always hear people say God makes mistakes that are a lie. From the beginning as scripture will tell you God created Adam and made Eve to multiply in this case having children.

The scripture tells us that Adam had rule over his wife Eve. She had to submit to her husband and fulfill his desires.

So women being submissive to your husband just simple mean follow and respect him as the head of the household. When a woman can submit to Jesus she will not have a problem submitting to her husband nor would she have problem respecting his authority. But he was not to take that authority and abuse it.

Disobeying God

When we disobey God and continue in sin He will utterly leave us to our destruction. God cannot and will not dwell in sin for He is a Holy God from Lev 19:2; 20:7; 20:26; 21:8; Exodus 19:6; 1 Peter 1:16 (NKJV). Everything God created is Holy even after Adam disobeyed God as I stated earlier. The LORD God does not see a fallen world He sees it as it was from the beginning and that's Holy through His son Jesus Christ The Anointed One.

Sin cannot stand in the presence of a Holy God. Our flesh is full of sin and the heart is deceitfully (dishonest, untruthful, lying (the Devil) above all things, and desperately wicked; (evil, sinful, immoral, and wrong) who can understand it "I the LORD search the heart and test the mind @to give every man according to the fruit of His deeds." Jer 17:9-10 (English standard Version) ESV

God knows the heart and thought of every man. He knew Adam would disobey Him and God had a back-up plan He sent Jesus to reconcile us back to Himself.

Furthermore, nothing that we do in this world surprises God because He create our hearts and mind to test us to see if we knew what's in it and how vile our mind we really are after all God said "For my thoughts are not your thoughts, neither are your ways my ways," declares the LORD. "As the heavens are higher than the earth, so are my ways higher than your ways and my thoughts that your thoughts.

Is 55:8-9 New International Version (NIV).

We talked about the marriage bed so I am gonna do this in a small way about marriage itself. Marriage is between a male and female. It is not for the faint in heart but mature adults only. It is not to be played with but to be taken seriously for God takes covenant to heart. That is why it breaks His heart to see men married the same sex as well as for women marrying women and how the laws allow this kind of behavior when God said it is an abomination. We have lost all respect for a God that can destroy the whole universe.

The world have Pride day just boasting about their sin and proud of it. How can anyone take pride in what they are doing against God? I get convicted every time I do something wrong. Of course I don't expect the lost souls to understand but when the light of God's word comes into play they will see only if the turn from their wicked ways. The often question that come to mind-What was I thinking to get involved in that? I've said it a couple of times. The point I am making here is I never tried is live for God but for man. Man will cause you separation from God and the devil wants your soul so he can go up against God. The sad part of it all is in the Book of Revelation 14:11 (NIV).

Fruitful, Multiply; and Deceived

Male and Female God created them to be fruitful and multiply to begin a family. The enemy has deceived the minds of the men and women to make them believe that they were supposed to be with the same sex.

I have even heard people say they were born that way. Let me put it this way the bible says John 8:44 NIV "You belong to your father, the devil, and you want out carry out your father's desires.

He was a murderer from the beginning, not holding to the truth for there is no truth in him, he speaks his native language, for he is a liar and the father of lies. He couldn't tell the truth if he wanted too and God never make mistakes what God meant for good the devil turn it to be evil.

The devil will never tell you the truth in the way you are living why because he wants your soul.

He wants to torment you making you believe that it is right to sleep with the same sex. He was a murder in the beginning when Cain slew his brother Abel and he still is a murderer now. The devil never changes his stripes.

He loves to play mind games and I have never seen so many gay, lesbians as much as I've seen on my job and they are increasing; it is like working in Sodom and Gomorrah now I understand what Lot must have been facing when he was living in the midst of a perverse generation

Now for the matter you wrote about "it is not good for a man not to have sexual relationship with a woman." 1 Cor 7:1 (KJV NIV)

This would easily be taken out of content. It is not good for a man to get intimate with a woman if he is not married to her. It is also clear that Paul is referring to a man and a woman. He not referring a man and a man getting intimate vice versa woman on woman.

If a man touches a woman he has defiled her it is a different when a man touches another man to God sin is sin but more so it's an abomination to the Lord to commit any sin.

The Marriage Bed

The man and woman when they are married share intimacy in their bed. They express how to love each other in a special unique way under God ordained purpose for the bed. The marriage is honorable among all, and the bed undefiled Heb 13:4. Nothing should corrupt a marriage bed. Let me say this bluntly; no man should ever sleep with the same sex or a woman with the same sex. This is not a marriage bed it is an abomination unto the Lord.

The marriage bed is not for fornicator or adulters God will judge. No husband nor wife should not take any one else to their bed it is considered committing adultery nor is the bed for fornicators this is having sex with a unmarried person.

The marriage bed is made for married couples only (male & Female). I have to abide by this as well. I will not go against God concerning these matters. It does not honor God when we go against Him it only separates us from Him.

The bible and the Merriam-Webster dictionary has the same meaning of what undefiled means-undefiled not corrupt, impure, or unclean, not defiled but the fornicators and adulters God will judge simply means if we are doing something unnatural out of wedlock God will judge.

Anything unclean going past God intention of a man and woman, sex immorality God will judge. This includes lesbians, homosexual, gay, bi-sexual etc. No stone will be left unturned the light will shine in the darkness of any area of our lives.

The word of God is to point out our short comings to put us in right position/standard with Him.   You will not find a scripture that will validate the behavior of human beings in their sin.

God did not give man to judge anyone according to their sins but he did say if we see our brother commit a sin we that are just restore such a person in the spirit of meekness but we were to be careful so we don't fall into the same sin and make sure we are free from that sin. Gal 6:1

Getting back to the word undefiled when a man sleep with the same sex the bed has become defiled as I read in my NKJV Bible study it say it as state earlier in Eccl 9:9 Live joyfully with the wife (you cannot call a man a wife or a wife a husband) who you love all the day of your vain life which has give you under the sun all your days of vanity; for that is your portion in life,

Once Jesus has enlightened us to word of God we ought to walk circumstantially into the light of the knowledge of God words we are without excuse.

<u>WIFE FOUND</u>

He who finds a wife finds a good thing. And obtain favor from the LORD. Proverbs 18:22

When I think about this scripture my mind goes back to the book of Genesis 3:18 when God said it's not good for man to be alone. He made him a helper that is equal to Adam a woman from his body. She became his wife, companion, best friend, and lover; mother of his children. That is what a male and female is all about living together as one unit under God's ordnance.

<u>He</u> (man) who finds a <u>wife</u> (woman) find a good thing; what does that mean a good thing. When God created the heavens and earth He always ending in saying it was good and that what a woman is all good for a man every curve of her body designed by a perfect God.

Someone who will walk closely by her husband side and He finds comfort in her presence and his trust is in her.

Favor: Problem in marriage arise from breakdowns in communication of mutual respect, not from some flaw in marriage itself v12:4 an excellent wife is a crown of her husband. But she who causes shame is like rottenness to his bone. **Excellent wife**, or "noble woman," are the same Hebrew words used in the famous acrostic in 31:10-31. A husband whose wife is like the woman described in chpt 31 should rejoice in her, because her noble character brings him honor. (NKJV) Study Bible.

Male, Female, Man and Woman opposite sex married but yet the same living together in harmony with the blessing of the Lord. Yes God kiss these couple and He (God) is pleased with His creation until the enemy corrupted the mind of Eve by deceiving her in Gene 3: 4-6 causing her to eat from the tree of the knowledge of good and evil.

Since Adam disobeyed God the enemy was able to pull man into utter darkness causing the eyes to desire everything opposite of what God attended it to be for that reason is why we have men and women sleeping with the same sex the enemy making it look good to them. And not only that but saying what he told Eve "You will not surely die v5 God know that in the day you eat of it your eyes will be opened and you will be like God knowing good and evil.

Adam and Eve didn't know anything about good or evil not until they ate from the tree of knowledge of good and evil then their eyes were opened. As stated earlier in the book Adam brought every living thing into total darkness. The eyes of many were blind to the fact that what we thought was rightful living was wrong according to the Bible (Jesus Gospel) revealed to us what good (which is God's Word) and evil (which is the devil works).

Fornication

For-ni-ca-tion- noun- sexual intercourse between people not married to each other. What does fornication mean in the Bible? To engage in premarital or extramarital sex, before or outside of marriage, is to sin in God's sight. That is precisely the point of Heb 13:4, a verse often referred to in this kind of discussion. (Wikipedia>wiki>fornication)

What are examples of fornication? (Noun) Fornication is defined as sexual intercourse between unmarried partners. An example of fornication is sexual intercourse between an unmarried man and an unmarried woman (YourDictionary>fornication)

What is fornication in Christianity? Fornication is any kind of sexual activity outside marriage, or between unmarried persons. We ought to keep our bodies holy, for the married, the bible says be faithful and for the singles keep yourself safe until you get married...if you cannot abstain yet you are a widow, **the bible** encourages to get married again. (May 12, 2018) http://www.newtimes.co.rw>what... What the Bible says about fornication the New Times.

Furthermore, fornication is general consensual sexual intercourse between two people again not married to each other. For many people the term carries an overtone of moral or religious disapproval, but the significance of sexual acts to which is applied varies between two religion society and culture- Resource fornication Wikipedia.

The bible in Col 3:5 "Put to death, therefore whatever belong to your earthy nature; sexual immorality, impurity, lust, evil desires and greed which is idolatry…Don't be greedy for a greedy person is an idolater, worshipping the things of the world (BibleGateway.com)

I heard this from a person I use to know and he said "If you entertain it long enough something is going to happen" Whatever comes to our mind we ought not to act on it. We ought to cast the thought down. The imagination of the mind should be brought under subjection. (2 Cor 10:5)

In the matter of divorcement when the Pharisees posed a question to Jesus about divorcing a woman. Jesus replied what did Moses decree or command you. And they said Moses suffered to write a bill of divorcement, and put her away. And Jesus answered and said unto them for the hardness of your heart he wrote you the precept but from the beginning of creation God made them male and female for this cause shall a man leave his father and mother (only reason a man leave his parents was when he was enter into a marriage) cleave t his wife. And they shall be one flesh: so they are no more twain but one flesh. What therefore God hath joined together, let no man put asunder. Mark 10:1-12 (KJV)

God put male and female together and it is the same as today. Society has change the very nature of what was suppose to the pure and made it impure, unholy, and unrighteous before the eyes of God.

On November 6, 2012, Maine, Maryland, and Washington became the first states to legalize same marriage through popular vote. (Wikipedia>wiki>same-sex_marriage) What is so popular about same sex marriage?

All twenty-eight state who passed state constitutional amendments that banned same-sex marriage to be legalized by judicial or legislative action: Alabama, Alaska, Arizona, California, Florida, Georgia, Idaho, Kansas, Kentucky, Louisiana, Michigan, Mississippi, Missouri, Montana,

Nebraska, Nevada, North Carolina, North Dakota, Ohio, Oklahoma, Oregon, South Carolina, South Dakota, Tennessee, Texas, Utah, Virginia, and Wisconsin. You can research more on this at LGBT rights in the United States-Wikipedia. En.m.wikipedia.org.

What we are now living in is a modern time Sodom and Gomorrah and the churches are being attack because they don't believe in same sex marriage and they refuse to perform anything such things that goes against God sanctity.

Jesus attended a marriage between a male and female John 2:1-11 in fact Jesus bless the water that turned into wine. You can read the scriptures at your leisurely time. Furthermore, as we move down in the chapters Roman 7:1-2 speaks about a woman being bound to her husband as longs as he lives, but when he dies she is released from that marriage

Let me sum this up for you fornication can be between an unmarried man and woman as well as same sex partners. Both are prohibited we are to present these bodies a living sacrifice holy unto our God that is our reasonable service to our Lord.

What is the punishment for fornication in the Bible? Lev 20:10 subsequently prescribes capital **punishment for adultery,** but refers to **adultery** between s man and a married woman: And the man that committeth **adultery** with another man's wife, even he that committeth **adultery** with his neighbor's wife, the adulterer and the adulteress shall surely be put to death. (http://en.wikipedia.org>wiki>Ad...).

Death was the punishment for committing adultery in the Old Testament as well as the New Testament 1Cor 6:9 (NIV biblehub.com) speaks about sexually immoral nor idolater nor adulterers nor men who have sex with other men. I'm gonna add a woman having sex with other women will not enter the kingdom of God either. Rev 21:8 has a list of other things that will not enter into the kingdom of God. Sin cannot dwell in the same place with a Holy God it hasn't in the beginning with Adam fall nor will it be in this present moment.

Then who can stand before our God? The one who has clean hands and a pure heart, who does not trust in idols or swear by a false god (NIV Ps 24:4) He that hath clean hands, and a pure heart; who hath not lifted up his soul unto vanity, nor sworn deceitfully (KJV)

~ 31 ~

Take Up Your Cross and Follow Him

Then Jesus said to His disciples, If anyone desires to come after Me, let him deny himself, and take up his cross and follow Me (Matt 16: 26a; Mark 8:34-38; Luke 9: 23-26). (NKJ Study Bible). Jesus as we know knew no sin but yet He sacrifices His life for ours and if we are to follow Him we must lay down our life and live His. Jesus endured the embarrassment of everything the people threw at Him from falsely being accused of blasphemy, being spit on, denied by Peter, beaten with thirty-nine stripes/lashes where His was flesh was torn off His body, punched in His face, clothes torn off of His body, carrying His cross, being nailed to it, buried and then brought back to life.

Can we stand to give up sin to go through what Jesus has gone through for us? Are we willing to leave everything we know that clings to our flesh give it up for Him? Every one of us falls short of the glory of God but yet we have a mediator who intercedes for us and His name is Jesus. What sin are you willing to give up for Jesus? These questions are for all of us. Are we willing to give up everything to follow Jesus or are we gonna stay in the sin that we're in. Is it worth us going to Hades for?

7 Do not be deceived, God is not mocked; for whatever a man sows, that he will also reap. 8 For he who sows to his flesh will of the flesh reap corruption, but he who sows to the Spirit will of the Spirit reap everlasting life. Gal 6:7-8
(NKJV STUDY BIBLE)

To make this easy and very clear for your understanding whatever we are doing wrong in the flesh or whatever we are taking delight in the flesh or feeding it that will we reap sickness, and diseases will be our corruption to the flesh. . Whatever we sow to the Spirit meaning doing something good, positive or constructive that pleases God we will reap everlasting life in other words live with our Heavenly Father.

Sin can make a big difference in our life it can destroy everything God has planned for us and takes us further away from God. Don't get me wrong He can use us for His glory and in the same breathe tell us to depart from Me you workers of iniquities I never knew you but for the saved He would say well done my good a faithful servant now enter in eternal rest.

Jesus Christ came to abolished sin when He can down from the Father to reconcile us back to Him (God) so that we will not walk after the flesh but the Spirit. Jesus has made all of us free from the law of sin but some of us have chosen to still fulfill the desire of the flesh and because of that you live according to the flesh.

Whatever you set your minds that will you; you do whatever a man thinks so is he. You are carnal (relating to physical, especially sexual, needs and activities) minded. Carnal is an adjective meaning "of the flesh." (Vocabulary.com>dictionary>carnal)

If we live according to the flesh we will spiritually die but if we put to death the deeds of the flesh will live for God. Read Roman 8: 1-17 at your conveniences.

As I stated earlier in the book what is not of God does not come from God it comes from the world and its lustful deeds and desires. It is so easy to recognize the difference between the Father and Satan. Every good and perfect gift is from above, coming down from the Father of the heavenly lights, who does not change like shifting shadows (NIV BIBLEHUB.COM). Satan is the opposite it is easy to recognize his bad deeds. I will sum it up like this everything in the flesh is from Satan. He knows nothing about being good. He comes to steal, kill and destroy everything that represents God. 1 Cor 2:14 (NIV BIBLEHUB.COM). The person without the Spirit does not accept the things that come from the Spirit of God but considers them foolishness, and cannot understand them because they are discerned only through the Spirit. But Jesus turned and said unto Peter, "Get behind Me, Satan! Your are a stumbling to Me; for you are not setting your mind on things of God, but on things of man (AMP version) That is why when we speak the things of God people look at us with a puzzled mind.

Cross Dressing

A woman shall not wear anything that pertains to a man, nor shall a man put on a woman's garment, for all who do so are an abomination to the LORD your God. Deut 22:5

Cross dressing was forbidden by Go in ancient Israel in the Middle East, dressing in the clothing of the opposite sex was a magical practice intended to bring harm to people. For example transvestite male would predict that the soldiers of another army would be as weak as females.

Women in the bible were not allowed to wear men trouser, shirts, and men suits; and ties let's not forget men shoes. In today's society this is what we are seeing more now than ever. Young ladies along with older woman are hanging their pants down off the butts and walking like a man. They're even cutting off their hair which is a woman's glory having different designs signet in printed on their heads.

God word will never change we are the ones that suppose and I say suppose to change to His word. He is not picking on us He is simply teaching us how we should live a godly life. He doesn't want us blind to the enemy's deception He's opening our spiritual eyes by exposing us to His word.

God fought for our soul through His Son Jesus Christ when He was crucified on the cross, died, and buried then on the third day He rose up with all power the same power He gave us to conquer sin. Then He (Jesus) left us with a comforter to help us on our journey to holiness. John 14:26 (JKV)

And if we take a step back for a moment and realize our lives is not our own we were brought with a price that we could never repay, and all God wants from us to do is one word and that's Obey.

Although I love Tyler Perry movies and plays in which I did get a laugh out of it not realizing I was condoning his behavior as a crossed dresser in his productions.

"Brother and sisters, if someone is caught in a sin, you who live by the Spirit should restore that person gently". Gal 6:1. We must consider ourselves before we can approach anyone to correct them. In other words make sure our back yard is clean before we try to correct someone in their trespasses and make sure we are not tempted with the same sin.

It is sad to see another Christian not restore his brethren back to Christ but yet accepts his donations for the church. We are about soul winning not taking their money and using it for the church which is a strange offering to God and not restore that person in the spirit of meekness.

Too many churches are taking money from the secular world and not winning their souls back to Christ. The wealth of the wicked is stored up for the righteous but not the way we think.

When God gave the spoils of the wicked they were destroyed. Which mean we are accepting spoils God says it's okay to accept? You catch that later on.

The story of Moses when God blessed the children of Israel He destroyed the enemies by drowning them in the Red Sea. Let's not forget how the possessed the land of Canann.

God do not have a respect of person when it comes to sin. He (God) has set forth precepts, commands and laws for a reason and if we trespass one we have trespass all.

As I grew deeper in the word of God I see how serious the word really is. It will wipe the smile off your face when you find out you were living in sin and what Mr. Perry was doing as a Christian man was sending mix message to our society of people who are going through identity crisis in which I will be discussing the in further chapters.

To sum this up we should be more concern about their souls than their money. We will never find Jesus taking money over a soul. Heaven rejoice over one soul. If we are not gonna do the will of the Father then some of us need to step back and allow the Remnant to take over and if the truth be told God is gonna use the Remnant to clean His house out starting with the pulpit.

~ 36 ~

Proper Dressing

I also want the women to dress modestly, with decency and propriety, adorning themselves, not with hairstyles or gold or pearls or expensive clothes but with good deeds, appropriate for women who profess to worship God.

1 Tim 2:9 NIV

And I want women to be modest in their appearance. They should wear decent and appropriate clothing and not draw attention to themselves by the way they fix their hair or by wearing gold or pearls or expensive clothes. For women who claim to be devoted to God should make themselves attractive by the things they do

1 Tim 2:9 NLV

Modest is someone or something that is humble or shy or not extreme. In this instance were gonna use the word extreme. Women ought to not overdue themselves by overdressing drawing the wrong attention with fancy clothing, hairstyles, gold or pearls. If they are trying to get a man's attention by her clothing, jewelry or hair style men who are truly in God don't fall for that it is the spirit that should attract a man. She should be dressed appropriately not showing any of her body parts.

Humble can be used if the women are listening to the Holy Spirit in which apparel is appropriate for church. God wants the heart and also the respect for His church.

Not to get off the subject of what a woman should or should not wear but to show that either way it is not acceptable in the Lord's eyes.

Whether a man or woman there are clothes for the right sex no man should be putting on women's clothes or vise versa.

A man is a man-a woman is a woman. I want to address this on a different perspective although Timothy addresses it this way a woman should look-not go all out to adorn their outer appearance to catch a man. I want to say this about this scripture women ought to put on women's apparel (clothing) she should not look like a man nor try to pimp their walk like one or wear men's cologne or shoes. God has made you female and He put a stamp on you and said "It's All Good."

Every time I put on my uniform for work in which I understand protocol I didn't feel like a woman all because we have to cover up our hair, we couldn't have long nails; if we got a manicure our nails had to be short understandable; no eyelashes were allowed; earrings couldn't be worn only wedding rings. That basically stripes a woman from being who she is intended to be. Its okay for a man to dress like that but for a woman it's a no, no.

There were women on my job who went against the rules of our company and did their hair that the net couldn't cover their heads not saying we couldn't do our hair it's that the net had to cover our whole head. Eyelashes looked like horse lashes; nails long where they couldn't search carts or carrier correctly half the time they broke their nails.

They were doing the right thing by looking like women but they were disobeying the rules of the company just like the woman of God.

When we do what we want or thing look good and not considered what God words dictate we sin. Dressing to be cute is not godly because God is not after cuteness He is after the heart. If God can get to the heart He got you and He will turn your life according to His Holy Word.

What is Proper Apparel For Women?

What is Proper Women's Dress (1 Timothy 2:9)? Cont

Related

<u>The Writing of Prostitutes</u>

The question of proper dress for women has been of interest to many. Actually, God's guidelines regarding clothing and dress are very general. God expects Christian women to dress in "modest apparel, with propriety and moderation (discretion, margin)" (I Timothy 2:9)—that is, in clothes that are not flamboyant and garish. A Christian woman should not be an "exhibitionist "in attracting undue attention to herself by wearing clothing that is provocative, suggestive, or outrageous. By the same token, this does not mean that Christian women should be drab, colorless, or tasteless dressers. A Christian is to be a light to the world (Matthew 5:14-16), an example of balance and good taste. We should not be so out of step with the fashions of society that west and out like the proverbial "sore thumb." Clothes can be fashionable without being immodest or peculiar. Apparel should be appropriate for the occasion—decent swimsuits for the beach, jeans for yard work, and usually a dress or other nicer outfit for special occasions.

A Christian woman should especially strive to look nice for her husband and family. In the Old Testament, God gives this law: "A woman shall not wear anything that pertains to a man, nor shall a man put on a woman's garment, for all who do so are an abomination to the LORD your God" (Deuteronomy 22:5). This refers to transvestitism or cross-dressing, not to a woman's wearing of pants that are designed for women. The simple principle is that men should look and dress like men—masculine—and women should look and dress like women—feminine. By doing so, we will both glorify God.

The "meek and quiet spirit" of a truly converted Christian woman will be reflected in the kind of clothing she selects (I Peter 3:1-4). She will wear what is appropriate and stylish for any given occasion, but with proper modesty and decorum. And God will look on the heart of such a woman with approval.

Gal 5: 19 Now the works of the flesh are evident which are adultery, fornication, uncleanness, lewdness 20 Idolatry, sorcery; hatred, contentions, jealousies, outburst of wrath, selfish, ambitions, dissension, heresies 21 envy, murders drunkenness, revelries, and the like of which I tell you beforehand, just as I told you in the past, that those who practice such thing **will not** inherit the kingdom of God. (Gal 5: 19-21 NIV)

Paul has given us a clear description of what will not enter the kingdom of God when we are practicing these things how much more will gay, homosexual, transvestite will enter in. You will never enter the Kingdom of God with sin.

The kingdom of God thrives on righteousness. God is Holy and no matter what nothing will enter Gods' kingdom any kind of way Jesus is the way the truth and the life no man comes before the Father but by him. (John 6:44). We must allow God to change our heart to be formed into His will.

Do not deceived God is not mocked; for whatever a man sows, that will he also reap 8 for he who sows (whatever you doing in the flesh) to the flesh will of the flesh reap corruption, but he who sows to the Spirit will of the Spirit reap everlasting life (simply will return home back with the Father)

For God did not send His Son into the world to condemn the world, but the world through Him might be saved (John 3:17) NKJV STUDY BIBLE

God sent His Son into this world to save us not condemn us. His blood covered a multitude of sin and without the shredding of blood there would be no remission of sin.

Jesus came down to the world to save us from sin. When He (Jesus) comes again He coming with a reward in his hand and judgment will be with Him only upon those who did not receive Him as the Savior.

Come now, and let us reason together, saith the LORD: thought your sins be as scarlet, they shall be as white as snow; though they be red like crimson, they shall be as wool (KJV) Isaiah 1:18

Salvation only comes to those who have received Jesus so no matter what we've done in our past Jesus came to erase it and give us a brighter future v3:18. To believe is to receive life vv15-16 and avoid judgment. He (God) wants to reason with all of us about the way we are living.

He want to clean us although our sin is disgustingly dirty God want to clean us white than snow anything whiter than snow is very bright where God don't see our sin anymore. Red as crimson represent murders hand stained with blood God will wash their hands as if they never sinned. Read Isaiah 1:15 - 18 New International Version for better understanding at your leisurely time.

When Jesus said "Come to me the way you are when I tell you "come as you are" It means come the way you are or how you are. It doesn't matter who you are or what you have done. Jesus is referring to the heart. He wants to change it and it didn't matter what color, culture or religion you believe in. Jesus welcomes everyone. It like the Army you never leave your man behind.

A person who does not believe not only misses eternal life, but is condemned already because simply you turned down the only Savior that could deliver you/us. The idea of believing in Jesus name is also found in v1:12.

Everything the bible describes in eternal. Returning back to the Father believing in Jesus is trusting Him in leading us by the Holy Spirit in which Jesus said He will send to lead us in all truth and if we refuse that truth the bible says we are already condemned because we didn't believe in the only begotten So of God.

All have fallen short of the glory of God but when we fall we have an advocate who stand in the gap for us the question is will we turn away from sin and receive Jesus as our advocate? Will we totally pick-up our cross and follow Him? Or will we allow our flesh dictate where we will spend eternity?

I would personally spend eternal life with Jesus my heavenly Father then to spend my life down here pleasuring my flesh.

The enemy has one mission is to kill, steal and destroy even the very hope we have in Jesus. The enemy wants to stop us from filling our God given purpose. Steal any chances that we have been given by God by sending his empts to block every opportunity that is presented to us.

Who is Preaching in the Pulpit

Speaking of the pulpit we have homosexual preaching the word of God if I recall there were no homosexuals leading God people in the Old or New Testament so how did this happen in this present time.

When the flesh has taken over it doesn't want to hear the truth of the word that would make us free 2 Tim 4:3 (NIV) For the time will come when people will not put up with sound doctrine. Instead, to suit their own desires, they will gather around a great number of teachers to say what their itching ears want to hear. In other that don't want to hear the truth like is said they only wanna hear it okay to live in sin and God love you anyway which is true God does love them but not their sin.

I remember one occasion not mentioning the church my Pastor was preaching on this subject and there were two lesbians sitting in the front of the church and one of them got convicted and want to live right for Jesus but the partner got upset and took her to the back of the church and we never say them again why because the enemy got scared of losing that soul so he kept her in her sin.

People only want to hear what they want to hear keep them bound and make them feel good they want us to say its okay when it's not so they find a church that's like them and never being made free.

Let me emphasize on this God can use that same homosexual and preach the word that will make them free. He has not respect of person but His word will get out there.

Remember what I said earlier God can use you and reject you at the same time.

Daily Bread

He is the way of life that keepeth instruction; but he that refuseth reproof erreth. (Proverb 10:17 KJV)

Inspiration

No man naturally walks in the way of life, nor can anyone simply figure it out on his own. All of us need the instruction found I God's Word in order to talk in the way that leads to life everlasting. If we refuse correction by God's Word, we sin against our won souls

Prayer

Teach me, O Lord, Your way; show me Your truths, that I man live. I would rather have the true spiritual life with You in abundance than to be exercised by the empty, fake "life" the world offers. I would rather a doorkeeper in the house of my God than to dwell in the tents of wickedness. (Psalm 84:10).

The Media

Media- the main mean of mass communication (broadcasting, publishing, and the Internet regarded collectively).

The media has a role in supporting certain thing we see on television some things they broadcast does not up-life the name of Jesus.

Many years ago you would never see commercial with homosexuals promoting HIV drugs with two men kissing each other for example the commercial Truvada. Dovato is another HIV drug they support with gay men. I don't have anything against the commercial but the sin it promotes is against the Word of God.

If we don't stand up for something we will fall for anything. I know people and even had friends who were homosexuals I had nothing against them but the sin. Jesus never had a problem with the people it was the sin He address. Like the woman at the well she had five husbands and the six one was not her but Jesus only told her what was going on in the life never once he called her an adulterous.

When the Jewish leader caught a woman in an adulterous act they brought her to Jesus and told him what she had done. Jesus responded by saying He who without sin let him cast the first stone. Nobody did they just departed Jesus looked around ask as the woman where are her accusers wondering why they didn't stone her. She said they left and he told her I don't condemn you either. She departed and told everyone all that Jesus had said to her concerning her life.

Like I stated early this book is not to condemn or judge but to correct the state of a person life. The word is designed for us to live the life God has for us.

Who is Jezebel?

Jezebel was the daughter of the priest-king Ethbaal, ruler of the Phoenician cities of Tyre and Sidon. When **Jezebel** married King Ahab of Israel (ruled c. 874-853 BCE), she persuaded him to introduce the worship of the Tyrian god Baal-Melkart, a nature god. Most of the prophets of Yahweh were killed at her command.

Jezebel has come to be known as an archetype of the wicked woman. According to the <u>Bible</u> (Kings I and II), she provoked conflict that weakened Israel for decades by interfering with the exclusive worship of the Hebrew god Yahweh, disregarding the rights of the common man, and defying the great prophets <u>Elijah</u> and <u>Elisha</u> .

Jezebel does not work alone she work closely with Belial, her daughter Athaliah, and Delilah. These demonic spirits were sent out by Satan when he wanted to annihilate someone life in other word what the low demon couldn't do or accomplish he sent out the big guns a whole different level of evil forces.

Jezebel is a destroyer of the church, community, and relationships, causes all kinds of chaos in marriage, she a spirit of adultery; controller, whoremonger, and deceiver and she is behind murder; homosexuality etc.

Reprobate spirits and spirits of homosexuality and lesbianism operate under the Belial cursing men to commit vile acts, thus bringing the judgment of God.

Until we all recognize that we are in need of a doctor we will continue to live and desire what the flesh is carving for but through the blood of Jesus we no longer live in sin but in the light of the word of God.

I always hear people say we already in Hades we are far from that if you read the book of Revelation.

God does not send people to Hades it is the desire of your flesh that brought God's judgment upon you and you sent yourself there. God said he wishes for no man to perish so how can God send someone to Hades.

As I stated earlier about the word if we live by the flesh we will fillfull the lust of the flesh.

Conclusion

In my conclusion of God Made Male and Female it is evident in His word that when God created man in His image and likeness the created them Male and Female to dwell together as Adam puts it Bone of my bone flesh of my flesh I shall call you woman for you came from man. God said they will no longer be two flesh but one.

They shall be to God Holy and respectable before Him. They shall be fruitful and multiply whatever they put their hand too. Male shall rule over the woman and woman will be submissive to her own husband.

God will bless the wife and her children as they submit to the head which is the husband. No blessing shall be held back as long as they walk in the statues of their God.

I expect there will be some argument about what is written in this book let me encourage you it is God's word and He will not change for us but we ought to change for Him to live in Holiness.

Sleeping with the same sex it not of God –what do darkness has to do with the light? 2 Cor 6:14 speaks about being unequally yoked and it not just for unbelievers who are hooked up with believers it for the homosexuals as well. What makes them unequally yoke sleeping with the same sex?

We have to understand that when God made man in his image and likeness He (God) had a woman on His mind. Gen 2:18, 20 -25) declares it. Which one of us knows the mind of God? (Isaiah 55:8 Rom 11:34, 1Cor 2:11) We will never figure out God as you read these chapters God is saying the same thing in the Old Testament and the New Testament. He's the same yesterday, today; and forevermore.

When you walk in darkness you will fall into destruction you will never know what God has for your life if you keep gratifying your flesh and I tend to believe that people really do like what they do in their flesh. I know I did until I found out it wasn't the way God intended for my life to be.

My God is full of joy, peace, love; and happiness and I am in pursuit of whatever God's has for me.

This book is written to put thing in its perspective order. It is time to take the scales of our eyes and live for God and not for man. Pride day is for God. Be proud of what God made you. A man is made for a woman and a woman is made for a man.

The bible is very clear about this and it should never be taking out of content to live the way either of us should live.

Let us not therefore judge one another anymore: but judge rather, that no man put a stumblingblock or an occasion to fall in his brother's way

Romans 14:13

As I stated earlier this book it no written to judge anyone but to correct our way of life. It is imperative that we exams our own selves to make sure we are in the right standard with God. We should never be a stumbling block if our brothers or sisters are struggling with sin. We who came through the sin their struggling with ought to help them get through it by praying for them. (Romans 15:1). For we are our brother keepers (Romans 14: 13-23) and we must make sure to take the beam out our own eyes instead of point fingers at the stumbler or we will be like a hypocrites in Jesus' time (Matt 7:5)

We ought to put on Christ knowing that the time we are living in is near for Christ Jesus to return. Let's go back to when we first believed and cast off the darkness of this world and put on the Armor of Light which is Jesus the Christ the Anointed, Holy One of Israel (Roman 13: 11-14).

God mercy does endure to all generation but why risk your life for one night of sinful pleasure when we can always run into Christ while His arms are still open wide, and the veil was ripped from top to bottom to give us access to God's Throne. Paul himself said shall me continue in sin where grace abound. God forbid No once we put on Christ we are dead to sin the old man has passed away all things were made new when Jesus went on the cross.

~ 48 ~

Everything died with him and when He (Jesus) rose up that was a newness of life that Jesus gave to us. He took the sting out death and now we walk in VICTORY so why should we be bound in sin any longer. (Roman 6: 1-12) a good read we should not take God's grace for granted the only time grace should be taking advantage of is when we are going through life circumstance, trials; and tribulations.

I want to give you this thought and it's scripture. What if Jesus comes back and we are caught in sin what would happen to us. I dread not to find out because the scripture does say no man know the hour nor time when Jesus is coming back not even Jesus don't know so why should we take that chance and lose our soul. (Matt 24:36-44, Mark 13:32, 1 Thess 5:1-2, Peter 3:10; and Rev 3:3)